HER LIMESTONE BONES

Her Limestone Bones

Selections from
Lexington Poetry Month 2013

Edited By

Hap Houlihan

and

Christopher McCurry

Accents Publishing • Lexington, Kentucky • 2014

Copyright © 2014 by Accents Publishing
All rights reserved

Printed in the United States of America

Accents Publishing
Editors: Hap Houlihan and Christopher McCurry
Cover Image: *Measure of a Man* by John Lackey (*homegrownpress.com*)
      courtesy of Tom and Becky Eblen
Cover Design: Simeon Kondev

Library of Congress Control Number: 2014936451
ISBN: 978-1-936628-24-7
First Edition

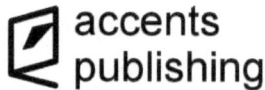

Accents Publishing is an independent press for brilliant voices. For a catalog of current and upcoming titles, please visit us on the Web at

www.accents-publishing.com

CONTENTS

From the Editors / ix

I. Lexington

SOUTHERN SEVERANCE / *Maggie Brewer* / 3
CHIAROSCURO / *Sherry Chandler* / 5
WE ARE THE GREEN NUDES / *Zachary Johnson* / 6
JOURNEYS—BLUEGRASS BACKROADS #2 / *Carole Johnston* / 7
THE MOST WONDROUS MUSICAL STAIRS … / *Kari Burchfield* / 8
I WALK TO WORK / *Alison Courtney* / 9
A HAIKU / *Clay Shields* / 10
KENTUCKY, I LOVE YOU / *Whitney Collins* / 11
THE MEETING ROOM, SHAKER VILLAGE / *Kristine Nowak* / 12
I'M ADDICTED / *Elane Moore-Turenne* / 14
WHAT TO DO DURING A SUMMER RAIN / *Karen George* / 15
THE WASP / *Christopher McCurry* / 16
KENTUCKY / *Beatrice Underwood-Sweet* / 17

II. In Love

'67 BLACK IMPALA / *Allie Marini Batts* / 21
YOU MET ME AT A STRANGE TIME IN MY LIFE / *Julian DeVille* / 22
MIRACLES / *Pauletta Hansel* / 23
FOR LAURA ON A SUNDAY AFTERNOON / *Matthew Haughton* / 24
SLIPPING BY / *Marta Dorton* / 25
A CHAIN OF CORRELATED CONSEQUENCES / *E. K. Mortenson* / 26
THE HEART IS A PERCUSSION INSTRUMENT / *Sayid R. Bnefsi* / 27
JELLYFISH / *Elizabeth Kilcoyne* / 28
MAD BOY'S LOVE SONG / *Bronson O'Quinn* / 29
TRICK / *Keith Stewart* / 30
A MIDNIGHT PSALM / *Jaria Gordon* / 31
MYRTLE'S REGRETS, ON THE ROCKS / *Savannah Sipple* / 32
SELF LOVE IS A MYTH / *Morghan Fuller* / 33
DROWNING / *Michelle Benningfield* / 34
AN HONEST QUESTION / *Corey Angel* / 35
BETTER YET / *Vijay Singh* / 36
NOT A TYPICAL MORNING / *Rudy Thomas* / 37

FRANK AFTER DINNER / *Jay McCoy* / 38
AFTER BREAKFAST / *G.A. Smith* / 39
IMPERFECT FIT / *Jennifer Beckett* / 40
DREAMS ARE STUPID ... / *Robin LaMer Rahija* / 41

III. With God

CULTIVATING REVERENCE / *Michelle Knickerbocker* / 45
EXCAVATING / *Bernie DeVille* / 46
THIS WILL REQUIRE AN APOLOGY / *Jason Lee Miller* / 47
TIME'S RODEO / *Karah Stokes* / 48
PURGATORY / *Mary Allen* / 49
MOMENTS / *Bront Davis* / 50
THE ANGEL OF EPHEMERA / *Jeremy Dae Paden* / 52
LOSS (ON FATHER'S DAY) / *Marianne Worthington* / 53
SUCCOR BLEU! / *Christopher Miller* / 54
SYNCHRONICITY / *Elle Wong* / 55
KNOW / *Betsy Packard* / 56
EVICTION / *Leatha Kendrick* / 58
SURVIVAL OF THE LUCKIEST / *Jay St. Orts* / 59
RETREAT / *Tyler Worthington* / 60
ZEN BALLOON / *Kate Spencer* / 62
REVERIE VIII / *Bianca Spriggs* / 63
HOW GOD PUNISHES / *Katerina Stoykova-Klemer* / 64

IV. On Poetry

STUCK, UNSTUCK / *George Ella Lyon* / 67
PREPARE TO CONTINUE / *M J Eaton* / 69
FOUND ART / *Sue Neufarth Howard* / 70
ANNE BRADSTREET'S KITCHEN / *Joanie DiMartino* / 71
BODY FLUIDS / *Nettie Farris* / 72
NOTHING TO OFFER / *Doug Self* / 73
CHANNELING MIYAGI / *Duke Gatsos* / 74
JUNE 3RD POEM / *Doug Jones* / 75
ELEVEN SEVERED FEET WASH UP ... / *Morgan Adams* / 76
FONDNESS / *K. Nicole Wilson* / 77
ODE TO THE SEMICOLON / *Deborah Adams Cooper* / 78
WITH POETRY / *Hap Houlihan* / 79

V. At Home

ON GOING HOME / *Teneice Durrant* / 83
OUT OF A RENTED EXISTENCE / *Pamela Gibbs Hirschler* / 84
ALL I WANT / *Jude Lally* / 85
COUNTRY BREAKFAST / *Davina Warner* / 86
UNCLE LEON / *Kevin Blankenship* / 87
FAÇADE / *Rae Cobbs* / 88
HOMELAND SECURED / *Michael Dean Benton* / 89
OEDIPUS COMPLEX / *Patrick Maloney* / 90
HOW A TEACHER PREPARES … / *Jason McKinley Williams* / 91
JAZZ PERSONAE POEM #19 / *Elizabeth Beck* / 93
THE LAST FOREIGN THING / *Jessica Swafford* / 94
GO WHERE MY BODY SAYS GO / *Melva Sue Priddy* / 95
WHAT TO DO WHEN YOU'RE LOCKED … / *Leigh Anne Hornfeldt* / 96

About the Poets / 99

About the Editors / 111

FROM THE EDITORS

Lexington, Kentucky: if you doubt the stubborn generosity of our mother ground, try to keep a bare patch in a Lexington garden. It will keep you busier than the rosebed and the honeysuckle hedge combined.

Lexington, Kentucky: if you're unfamiliar with our adornments, try these helpful keywords: Arboretum, Bourbon, Chevy Chase, Dudley's, Elkhorn Creek, Farmers Market, Gratz Park, Horses, et cetera. Any true Lexingtonian can cobble together an A-to-Z list for you.

Lexington, Kentucky: if you're unacquainted with our people, well, that's fair: we have as many adjectives as citizens. This plurality enriches Lexington and attracts new people. But if you listen closely (if you're reading this book, your ears are working just fine), you will begin to detect a Song—behind, above, and amidst the slow noise of Lexington streets. The Song voices our laments and exultations, it encompasses dissonance and harmonies, and it's getting louder all the time.

It is the Song of Lexington's cultural character. The longer you listen to the Song, the more likely it is that you'll find yourself singing along, adding your own measures and phrases. This collection is a libretto of sorts, describing a small portion of the Song. More verses of our Song can be found in the work of the other poets who contributed during Lexington Poetry Month.

You are encouraged to explore the trove from which these poems were selected: the Lexington Poetry Month blog. Over eighty writers from (or otherwise attached to) Lexington wrote a poem each day in June 2013, posting those pieces that met their satisfaction. The results—over one thousand poems—are distinctive yet harmonious. Lexington Poetry Month is a new chorus in the Song, one that will be sung anew each June in Lexington.

—*Hap Houlihan and Christopher McCurry*

The Lexington Poetry Month 2013 blog can be found at:
accents-publishing.com/blog/category/lexington-poetry-month/

ND OF PDF DOCUMENT.
I. Lexington

SOUTHERN SEVERANCE
Maggie Brewer

Before I moved here I had
never seen a
blue heron
standing in a pond
wrapped in a layer of fog.

Never heard a mandolin
or bluegrass music played
up on the stage,
under the stars.

Never tasted
cold, crisp Ale-8.
Bottle opened
against the edge of the counter.

Never heard a
turkey call
so familiar now,
or deer antlers
knock at night.

Never savored
mint julep,
bourbon balls,
or homemade
pimento cheese.

Didn't know tobacco
in all its incarnations;
beauty and life and death.
Tobacco stick,

tobacco worm,
tobacco barn.

Didn't know a waller from a holler,
how a camera could make a picture,
a teacher could take up an assignment,
I could make a grade.

But then my heart had never smiled,
or been loved a blue million,
or not cared to do something
and meant
I didn't mind.

CHIAROSCURO
Sherry Chandler

So I'm stopped at the light, North Broadway and New Circle, when a couple of Harleys pull up beside me: his and hers. His was fire-engine red with dual exhaust, hers metal-flake green with white sidewalls and a heavy load of chrome. The riders' spread on the seats was not that of youth. Besides they both had helmets on, though his had a ponytail of American-flag bandana hanging out behind. I never had the nerve to ride a cycle. I blame Jimmy Black who taught me to ride a bicycle by taking me to the top of the Pawpaw Tim hill and giving me a shove, and I knew I couldn't hit that gravel, blurring by as the bike picked up speed, with my bare arms and legs. Brakes never entered my terror-frozen mind. "I'll teach you to ride a bike," he'd said. "You promise you won't let me fall," I'd said. "I won't let you fall." I didn't fall. I'd like to say I never quite trusted anyone again after that summer but once naïve always naïve. A year or so later, I did take a spill on that hill and the doctor spent an hour picking limestone pebbles out of the hole on my knee, all the while scolding me for popping my gum. I can show you the scar.

WE ARE THE GREEN NUDES
Zachary Johnson

in Gratz Park. I am holding a sailboat, smiling
at your perky breasts. You perch—serenely enthralled
swatting the Fifth Third Bank away from the Carnegie
Center into cumulus clouds all shrouded in ash

leaves. Here, in Gratz Park, without regrets, I would have
loved you—frozen within this Fountain Dedicated
to Youth—forever. We as ice; old copper. Our image
—a gift to the children of Lexington. Our offering

—Eros over broken water pipes that surge
like tapering piss-streams while pursed-lipped
fogies traipse around and admire us. Trapped
in endless adolescence.

    for JML

JOURNEYS—BLUEGRASS BACKROADS #2
Carole Johnston

going where
the road slows down
my heartbeat

no one cares if
I stop the car to watch
a deer grazing

no honking
horns rush me
to move on

the day is wide open
pure blue sky honey solstice
I turn the radio off and

listen to the grass

THE MOST WONDROUS MUSICAL STAIRS OF P.O.T.
Kari Burchfield

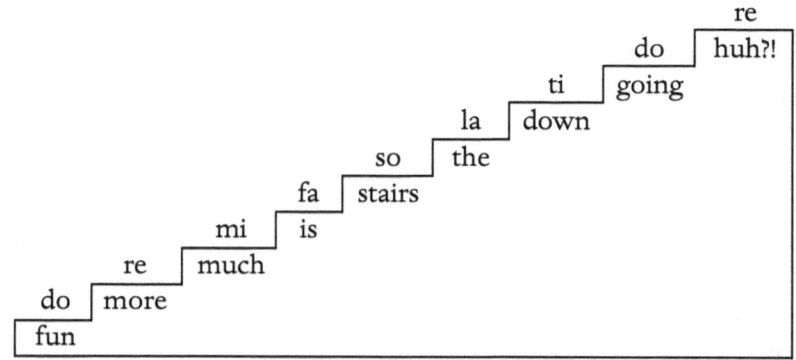

I WALK TO WORK
Alison Courtney

My feet take me onto Tates Creek Road
And the cars become louder, especially
The ones that run the light, and I give them
A mental finger and a sarcastic thumbs-up

The same light where the green Mini
Swings onto the road at 9:53
Past me and and past the shrieks of recess
That he can't hear in his little box

There's the corner where the momma possum
And her babies left a stain for months
An oily skidmark the only reminder
Of roadkill, the smell long gone

Here's the church, and the steeple
I don't open the door to see all the people
Because it's Tuesday and Greek dinner night
Only happens once a month on Fridays

The commuters can't see what I can
The worms, as if the sky rained them down
The empty pack of cigarettes and the
Broken porn DVD all scratched and cracked

Or the possum and her pups, first bloated by decay
Then slowly flattened into the pavement
One set of tires at a time, their meat battered
Until the stink was gone but the stain remained

A HAIKU
Clay Shields

My Eastern Kentuck
jumps the dam and I holler,
"That's a green ass hill!"

KENTUCKY, I LOVE YOU
Whitney Collins

Kentucky isn't really in
The Southeast
Or Deep South
Or Midwest
Or Northeast
Or Mid-Atlantic
Or Plains States
Or High Plains

It's just there

In the middle

Like Jan Brady

Like Jan Brady
Drinking good bourbon
Straight from the bottle

And giving everyone the finger

In a nice, friendly sort of way

THE MEETING ROOM, SHAKER VILLAGE
Kristine Nowak

If sound echoes, then it must echo forever—
softer with each iteration, the more delicate
the ear needed to catch it.

In every place where there was
singing and dancing and stomping,
there must be some faint

reverberation
that gets closer to silence,
but never reaches it.

The room where they sang
is all clean benches now,
a great stage of empty

and gleaming floor,
windows that cast rivers of sun
across the barren wood.

I could swear
there is nothing here—
not even ghosts.

But somewhere under this veneer
of silence, there must be dozens
of voices pounding to song,

there must be heavy footfalls
that shake these same windows.
There must be more

than these lone lines of light
and shadow tracking time
across the floor.

I'M ADDICTED
Elane Moore-Turenne

I'm addicted to coffee at Mickey D's.
Don't say, "It's not healthy."
   I know how to please and I
   know what satisfies me!

You can buy Starbucks or
   grind your own beans,
But I know the taste I need
   to be pleased.
There's nothing for me but
   my coffee at Mickey D's!

WHAT TO DO DURING A SUMMER RAIN
Karen George

Carry houseplants outside, take
a walk without an umbrella,
let the rain cascade
down your arms, face,
feel your hair go limp,
then heavy as it absorbs,
the way wet socks squish.

Remove your glasses,
fold and tuck them in a pocket,
everything fuzzy at first.
Guzzle scents of wet
soil, leaves, concrete.
Visualize how robins
will pull worms from the earth,
how pill bugs will revel beneath rocks.

THE WASP
Christopher McCurry

This was a standoff. I had my Ale-8 sweating in hand. She had her red-molten body and my steering wheel. I've been crushing ants, I told her. Killed a black widow, too. (A lie: my mother killed it when she found it in an overturned flowerpot). Still, I had all day—though some high school kids were eyeing me and my green tank top and salmon shorts from the parking lot. When she finally flew off, I jumped in my car, started it up, and smashed my fingers onto the buttons to the electric window (Did I mention the windows were down!) and as the gap closed steadily but slowly, she rushed the crack; I yelled, recoiled, moved to defend my eyes with the Ale-8, spilling it into my lap. If not for that, it would have been a flawless victory. I even decided to stare down those high schoolers, when I flicked the severed head from the window.

KENTUCKY
Beatrice Underwood-Sweet

Her limestone bones
hold up the Appalachians.
Her curves are sexy hollers,
knobs and hills.
Every day she dresses
in Derby finery,
as blue-green as her grass,
hat tipped coyly
over one eye.
Not all her secrets uncovered yet.
Bourbon ferments in her veins
while Thoroughbred foals gambol
at her feet, dreaming of races
and wreaths of roses.
A graceful Southern lady,
crumbling stone fences
girding her spine.

II. In Love

'67 BLACK IMPALA
Allie Marini Batts

aggressive
as the bad-boy leather jacket
but better cared for,
quarter panels polished
& tipped in chrome

tilt the wheel
flat-palmed, one-handed,
shift gear & I moan in V6
while my second skin of denim Levis
sweet talks the swell of his bucket seat

way past curfew,
shimmy down the drainpipe
& run spaghetti-legged to meet him,
joyride till dew & dawn

gloss the hood of a car
I will always
miss more
than I miss him.

YOU MET ME AT A STRANGE TIME IN MY LIFE
Julian DeVille

I have adolescence chained up in my basement
but am unsure what to do with it
it only speaks in hisses and shadowy vapor
it dissents to all it hears
anything will hurt it, and everything angers it
I'm not sure if it's dead and seeks life
or if it's alive and seeks death
it is the only thing I know
that honestly does not want to exist

MIRACLES
Pauletta Hansel

I am complaining again
about miracles
this morning, the birds
who know exactly where
I tamped down
cosmos, zinnia, cockscomb
sunflower seeds in what I call
the garden (they call
tuwhee, tuwhee)
and how those seeds will
end up who knows where,
splatted on car windows, yes,
but maybe in some other
woman's garden, sprouting
among her squash and beans—
Honey, she'll call,
*did you plant these
flowers for me?*

FOR LAURA ON A SUNDAY AFTERNOON
Matthew Haughton

After refilling her cup of tea,
I return
to observing
as she reads
Katherine Mansfield.
This morning,
we caught Peter Pan
on the the television.
Wendy was busy
sewing the poor boy's
shadow to his sole.
Only just awake,
My Tigerlily
could still recall
every song.
Now the only singing
comes from
sunflower seeds
crunched by her teeth.
And the long sips
that come
as she enjoys her tea.
The light
invading as it does,
slips over the carpet.
Where no doubt
I will soon fall asleep,
listening as she reads.

SLIPPING BY
Marta Dorton

12:33
the time quickly approaches
I lie in bed and watch
red digital numbers update to 12:34

I always think of him then
he used to say that he saw 12:34
on the clock twice a day
our son and I pay homage
to his memory
when we see that number

I felt I had missed his spirit
one minute past 12:34
like a missed opportunity or guest
I anguished in another loss
as if I could have a conversation
or personal experience
had I been aware of 12:34
and him

more often the time slides by
unnoticed, twice a day
as the weeks and years roll on
12:35

A CHAIN OF CORRELATED CONSEQUENCES
E. K. Mortenson

But in this world, time cannot be doubted: it proceeds
in reverse, thereby making our last moment the moment
that we met; the gorgeous frantic spring of arrival when
so much is about to begin. This is how we part: not
in fading darkness, obscured to each other, but staring
at the sun, retina-burned by love's newest blaze. An ending

that allows us to question: will this continue, or is it a memory.

THE HEART IS A PERCUSSION INSTRUMENT
Sayid R. Bnefsi

you came so
suddenly to the room,
my heart became a gong
and was bashed just
to honor your entrance.

JELLYFISH
Elizabeth Kilcoyne

The boy I think you are sleeping with has brown eyes
and he won't look up at me   when he talks.
I am fiddling with a straw wrapper, waiting and trying
not to feel like I stained something expensive
tipping over   someone else's glass of wine.

You are probably sleeping with this boy wearing blue jeans
and sitting two seats away   from you
because he is listening to you talking while he is talking to me.
He watches you picking at a scab on your wrist.
You squeeze lemon into your water and his eyes are there.

If this is the boy you have been sleeping with, I understand
your want of a clean love—   like soap in your hand.
He is still enrolled in university studying something hopeful.
He wears pastel dress shirts and forgets to tuck them in.
Your hands feel safe pulling at the waistband of his jeans.

I know that you will take this boy in time and break him down,
until his lips tremble when you kiss him, until his hands shake
a staccato   he will try to still, pressing them to your spine.
This isn't your fault—   you didn't ask to be a neurotoxin
to bleed boys like leeches latching onto their unmarked skin.

But when his mouth twitches up at the touch of your smile
I remember the way the poison of you sets in.

MAD BOY'S LOVE SONG
Bronson O'Quinn

You, starry-eyed, became more than a name.
A raving angel cursed with peace of mind
Who traveled back along the path you came.

I shut my eyes and nothing stays the same
Yes, words can only pierce the fog, I'm blind.
You, starry-eyed, became more than a name.

If darkness wins, then tell me who's to blame.
I can't walk far without a path to find.
Then traveled back along the path I came.

When demons dance while angels are aflame
And Satan laughs when holiness resigned
You, starry-eyed, become more than a name.

Because St. Peter should be filled with shame
When posthumous reprieve is undefined
And sends you back along the path you came.

But still, you should be left with peace of mind
Just knowing what it was you left behind.
You, starry-eyed, are more than just a name.
You traveled back along the path you came.

TRICK
Keith Stewart

We rest in the darkness
of the glaring new moon.

Our bodies meld,
long-missing puzzle pieces
glued together by sweat
and hunger.

My desire is so devastating
I wish I'd used my real name.

A MIDNIGHT PSALM
Jaria Gordon

as i lay me
down to sleep
i pray my legs
won't spread my grief
into a roaming field he'll lay
to desecrate and soil beneath

the mourning comes
with weeping grace
i the sheep pasture-flung
desperation tousled sheets
trying to belt
last night unsung

with honey bourbon
corn flakes and dry heaves
i notch his belt, he unties my feet
and i pray the lord
didn't see me hung
from bed post sacrificially

a naked beast
drunkenly hungering along
alive but asleep and as i wake
if i do wake
i pray my soul
he won't forsake

MYRTLE'S REGRETS, ON THE ROCKS
Savannah Sipple

He drank in my loneliness at the bar,
threw it back like straight bourbon, with a slant
in the right corner of his mouth. It was the snap
of his head, the ways his eyes caught mine
as the glass slammed down that made me
follow him to the bottom of the barrel.

SELF LOVE IS A MYTH
Morghan Fuller

Nineteen years old and I have never smiled at my own reflection.
Society has told me that self-love is just conceited, and that it's not okay to feel pretty.
I have spent years picking apart every feature, and keeping track of everything that's wrong.

Lip size, hair line, the sound of my own voice.

There are campaigns teaching girls to accept their weight,
But I'd be so much happier if my obesity was all there is to hate.

DROWNING
Michelle Benningfield

is not a great splash
cries for help
arms flailing
slapping the water
it's a quiet event
the person beside you
on the couch
will never hear a sound
when you go under

AN HONEST QUESTION
Corey Angel

heat crawls along

your skin
as weightless centipedes
the blush on her cheeks
melts towards her chin
she turns to you
forehead burned pink
how far can a human fall
and still survive   she asks

touching her toes to the edge

of the roof
you remember him
pushing his fingers
between her thighs
under the kitchen table
you think
        a long way

BETTER YET
Vijay Singh

In the soft light of dawn
Wind across the river flows
Rhythmic lap of water on shore

Now the sun rises on the horizon
Streak of light on water sparkles
Sound of music in my ears roars

That is all the reality there is;
About as good as it gets
And it is good enough

Still, it would be an improvement,
If we were as romantic as in our youth
And you were here to share this moment

NOT A TYPICAL MORNING
Rudy Thomas

On this
not a typical morning
I sit on the edge of the bed
while it is yet dark
& I long to touch you.

After daylight
on this
not a typical morning
I work out at the gym
with a group of students.

I skip breakfast
on this
not a typical morning
& create a butterfly on the painting
I thought was finished.

On this
not a typical morning
I remember my brother
& how in his dying
he told me he loved me

for the
first
last
& only time
in our lives.

FRANK AFTER DINNER
Jay McCoy

On those mornings
as he awakens,
he whispers so
lowly. So close, he
nibbles my ear
as if it were
buttered sweet corn
still on the cob.
All he needs now
is a little more
salt.

AFTER BREAKFAST
G.A. Smith

carrying plates stained
with egg flakes, strawberry juice,
cinnamon jewels, I stop at
the doorway, walk back
to the bed you helped me
with pulling the sheet taut,
reach behind the pillows
and untie my belt
from the head board,
and we smile like the trick
we're about to play across
the spades table,
then head down the hallway.

IMPERFECT FIT
Jennifer Beckett

Traces of earned sweat
salt skin. This heart licks, laps
its lips, grows stronger
in abandonment. Lungs expand to hold
the atmosphere. I overcome. Sometimes

the most strenuous exercise is walking

away.

DREAMS ARE STUPID AND DON'T MEAN ANYTHING
Robin LaMer Rahija

There was an object
and a closet

I couldn't reach
so you took it and put it
on the top shelf.

In doing so
your body leaned
against my body
into the closet

and that was it
and everything.

I know from this omen
I'm in love with you
a little bit
in the way grown
out of distance
from the nuances
of your body.

Or else not.
It was a dream.
Touching is confusing
in real life and in sleep.

But we were kinder
to each other than we'd
ever been before.

This is the true sin
of my desire for you.

III. With God

CULTIVATING REVERENCE
Michelle Knickerbocker

Waking early, Sunday morning;
it didn't matter that we'd remembered
to turn the alarms off.
I rise,
even before the dog
has stirred from slumber.
Sneaking out back in bare feet
the deck is still damp.
Gently touching our tiny tomatoes
I imagine for just a moment
I know how a parent feels
standing over the crib
watching my baby sleep and grow.

EXCAVATING
Bernie DeVille

I am the eldritch resurrectionist of lost things,
a dream archeologist, a slovenly backpacker of the imagination,
creating a catechism of the miscellany of youth
from the rusted, toothy bottlecaps pulled from the earth of memory.
Come tour the little time tomb, the atrocity exhibition
of one who knows the gnawing gravel of fear in the stomach,
the butterfly collector, the boneshaker of the extinction machine.
Unrolled, the map I'm making is thematic, not linear.
In the blank places though, there still be monsters.

THIS WILL REQUIRE AN APOLOGY
Jason Lee Miller

Buddha and Jesus walk into a bar
Just to hang out, maybe shoot some pool
It's a nice place, tolerant, upstairs
Barkeep says they're running low on Jack
He's instantly wrong, now holding a full fifth
Buddha cracks up, one-hand-claps Jesus on the shoulder

They grab a couple cues
Jesus racks; he insists
Buddha breaks, silently, without violence
The balls scatter, hit the pockets
        Four sets of two
        One set of three
        And the eight ball in a final set of four
Buddha smiles
But Jesus makes him scratch

TIME'S RODEO
Karah Stokes

The moon is in a killing sign today. It says, Don't touch
the things you want to thrive, the things you love.

But they touch me. The sounds of spring
roll through me like ripples in a pool. A bee
hums loud inside a viola half its size,
wrestles like a bucking bronc for gold
it finds there. The breeze strokes waves into the grass,
strokes velvet petals, strokes waves on me.
Leaves brush my feet. The cat twines round my legs
on her way to scratch her back on sun-warmed stone.

So I'll defy the moon. I'll touch
all the things I love. I'll smooth the ground
I plant, I'll brush the velvet petals. Nuzzle
for the incense inside violas. I'll touch the sounds
and they'll touch me. I'll stroke the fur. I'll clasp
the hand. I'll pat the arm. I'll caress and slap
the clay. I'll clutch this pen
like a lover I can't let go. Tonight
I'll lay my hands with care on someone sleeping.

The moon might be surprised. With time,
its edicts can be twisted. What's wrong right now
is right sometimes. Time's a rodeo,
and I know how to ride.
I stick like cockleburr.
I'll stick my wrongest ways
until their time comes right.

PURGATORY
Mary Allen

She sits, strapped in her chair, gazing
toward the narrow swath of grass
the brochure terms The Garden.
Save for the incessant twitch
of her left hand and the rhythm
of her shallow breath, she does not move.
On good days she is silent, subdued. On bad,
she babbles and shrieks in a language known
only to herself and spits back the pabulum
proffered by the hesitant aid. Despite efforts
of staff, she often smells of stool.
Long ago, after visiting Aunt Belle, she said to me,
If I ever get like that, take me out and shoot me.

MOMENTS
Bront Davis

Moments are not minutes
Minutes seem minute, suitable only
For traffic jams and standing in line

It is with minutes we count
The in-between, the travel-time
The minutiae

Minutes only add up to hours
The material of our lives, perhaps
The space in which to live,
But not the moments

The moments resist classification
They are singular, unstrung
There is the moment of birth and
The moment of death
The moment when you first realize love is
Not only possible but deep
Or the moment of waking
And finding that, despite all the likelihood,
You were still alive (the moment of death postponed)

And these are the profound times,
Times when one is caught up
Not in time but in some other, rarer, medium

However, I've come to reckon that
The store of minutes allotted me is diminishing
And that possibly I've wasted more minutes
Than those I have remaining

I've become a seeker of moments
Not content to wait for them
But looking for them
Learning how to see them

True, moments not so momentous as
Birth or death, but still
There is the light reflected on
The deep waters of gratitude

THE ANGEL OF EPHEMERA
Jeremy Dae Paden

has no truck with collectors
of programs & ticket stubs
political buttons & fans

not from professional jealousies
but ethics, for those that scour
flea markets & basements

passing over the handmade
playbill for a punk band
that never left the garage

are like galleries that hack off
graffiti from walls before soot
& grime & errant taggers touch it

the Angel of Ephemera
moves about in silver robes
with wings slight as a dayfly

it hovers close to telephone poles
rises out of the memory box
of an eight-year-old girl

who knows that nothing
is truly evanescent, that all
things matter & leave their mark

LOSS (ON FATHER'S DAY)
Marianne Worthington

I watch for keen blue lines
on the legs, the arms, the penis,
forerunners that speak my name.
I am not grim, never angry, no
angel. Just the one to deliver
a crippled body back to dirt.
I am the sigh in the corner
of a sick room, the rattle
in the breath.

SUCCOR BLEU!
Christopher Miller

Sometimes
it is best
not to pray.

A tabled
plea for help
is enough

without the
added burden
of knowing

divine favor
was willfully
witheld.

SYNCHRONICITY
Elle Wong

we are living accidents.
we have died in rooms as large as God
and as small as empty bowls;

life does not compromise
for people like us—our souls
are compromised by it,

fish to flesh, hundreds
of teeth tilling our stomachs
until we tuck the drooping guts back

inside; because we don't see
accidents, only the terrible moons
of our shrinking hands—our wicked tools

destroying, collapsing, and gnawing
at planets—always eating
too much. there are a million excuses

for everyone else, but none
for yourself. and so you breathe through life—
only breathing. the rest

is too much. but like hogs, we root
our hooves through the mud, staring down
the universe. and we are still accidents—

we are so accidental, so starry and nebulous
and broken—hurting, hurtling towards
our own suns. we are beautiful,

beautiful little mistakes.

KNOW
Betsy Packard

Dust explodes from his sandaled   feet
as he doubles to catch the
   tourists.
"Your hand, madam," he pleads,   bowing.
"Give me your hand," he reaches.
"No, no money."
"Please, no money."
He shows them his palm
stopping the man from
   excavating in pockets.

"You," he says
gently turning his outstretched
   hand,
beckoning.
"I must tell your fortune.
Give me your hand."
He lunges, grasping air.

She clasps both hands
behind her back.
She shakes her head.

"I must tell fortune," he demands.

"No," she says.

"You say, 'No,' madam?" he asks.
"You say, 'No'?"

"I say, 'No,'" she says
as fear tugs at her chin.

"No," she says again.
"I really shouldn't know."

EVICTION
Leatha Kendrick

Most of what
I lost I took
from myself.

SURVIVAL OF THE LUCKIEST
Jay St. Orts

I sit in my neurologist's office,
Staring out the window
At the place where I spent a month
In rehab, fighting for my life
I cannot stop looking,
As I feel—really feel,
Tangible as a headlock—myself staring back
From my hospital room
The wounded me across the street
Knows nothing of the other me,
Other than he desperately wants
To be where I am

RETREAT
Tyler Worthington

Here's the story of a painter
delightfully eccentric
whose favorite place
to sit and paint
for to him
it was quaint
he would say
"perfect, perfect as rain"
was an insane asylum
named after a saint

who or which one
he always forgot
the road of gravel and dirt
leading to his studio
it's still lined with willow trees
haphazardly growing this way and that
across the lawn over the hill
far from the nearest town
old enough to have seen a few wars
old enough to welcome the kids
who couldn't kill

meet the locals
they're an interesting bunch
for example the gentleman there
see him by the pond
Bartholomew is his name
he's taking his lunch
and feeding half of it
to his pet snapping turtle

how they established their friendship
remains a local mystery
nice fella
his vocabulary is a bit limited
not a big talker
but very kind

feel free to sit out front for a spell
drink some tea
relax and sigh
and thank the Lord for feeling
and once more for feeling well
can't wait to see what the painter has made today
an abstract a landscape
who knows
he's a jack of all trades
sitting in the tallest room
suits him just fine
I guess there's more to loneliness
than meets the eye

ZEN BALLOON
Kate Spencer

Lighter than air
by definition

A celebration.
Colorful, round
Ready to burst

with expectation?
with possibility?
with happiness?

Yet …

Tethered.
Attached.
Unable to be free

Grasped.
Clutched.
A fear of letting it be

What it is.

Anguish, despair
at the thought of loss.
Until …

A new delight
the sight
gently lifting, floating free.

Peace in letting go.

REVERIE VIII
Bianca Spriggs

It's almost as if you don't wish to see them, their amber and onyx bodies lying curdled on the blacktop, weathered as ancient coins, and still as winged seeds left abandoned by the wind. Maybe a thousand dead bees blown from their man-made hives up on the roof down into the parking lot. You mouth a prayer for every one we step over. Crossing an acre of asphalt never took anyone so long. By the time we reach his door, the old terrapin has turned his sign over from "Open" to "Closed," but you knock anyway until he answers. He invites us in only because it's you, using his armored lips to turn the knob. We recline on velvet floor pillows as he prepares us a platter of his famous homemade sauerkraut, swatting away the fireflies who seem to love his sauerkraut too. His oblong eye wanders over, and he asks me frankly what we are doing there since he forgot how to tell the future long ago. I want you to answer, but you have fallen asleep in the corner, stuffed with sauerkraut and spirits, and by the time I can think of what to say, his breath, which smells of sandalwood, drifts through the evening haze like low-hanging fog and I forget. *I want to know where all the bees go when they die,* I say instead. He must not have heard, because he's retracted into his shell, and the voice of a hammered dulcimer wanders out. The fireflies lilt in time, singing along in tinny breathy whispers. And there are so many of them, maybe a thousand bioluminescent bodies, I believe that now, maybe I know.

HOW GOD PUNISHES
Katerina Stoykova-Klemer

You have an important question
You ask, and receive
The answer at once
You don't like what you hear
You ask again
And again until
You pick up a response that pleases you
There
Now you know
What to do

IV. On Poetry

STUCK, UNSTUCK
George Ella Lyon

I came to the stuck place.
I nudged. I coaxed.
I mocked. Walked away.

Back at the stuck place
I cursed. I railed.
I blasted. No go.

Then I sat down
at the stuck place
and wept.

In tears
the obstacle
dissolved

or was carried
out of sight
around the bend.

I came again
to the stuck place.
Such anger! Such
righteous refusing
to budge. I won't
give in to the stuck
place. I won't give
in. I will it to move
I will

be stuck.

The obstacle laughed
itself loose, rolled on
downstream.

Oh, honey,
Cry   Laugh   Keep moving

PREPARE TO CONTINUE
M J Eaton

Read and reread
The classics
On a
Regular basis.
Glean from them
As though new.
Cherish the time
Away from writing
Filling the vehicle
That will run for you
Until your words
Come as though
New in your hands.

FOUND ART
Sue Neufarth Howard

Black
and white
abstract, one
hundred ants in
geometric lines
on the pavement;
something sweet
and sticky
there.

ANNE BRADSTREET'S KITCHEN
Joanie DiMartino

this must be where Anne
wrote her poems each rhyme bubbled
up like hungry yeast then softened
plied with rye flour
while dry wood in the beehive oven
crackled and flared
scorched the inner brick walls
with alabaster soot
first lines folded into puffs of flour
clouds released as palms pressed
then nimble fingers
pivoted swift quarter-turns
of thick oval bread mixture
repeat   repeat   repeat
the sweat on her skin the sharp pleasant
pain in her arm muscles
from this rhythm of kneading
after first rise
before her quill scratched
on thick paper a day's worth
of gathered fragments
whiffs of moist dough
ebbed and flowed
like Boston Harbor's tides

BODY FLUIDS
Nettie Farris

Viscosity announces itself as
the word of the day. Lemonade with extra pulp calls your name before you even
leave the bed. Thick, local honey sweetens
your green tea, and the vascular system,
meantime, intrigues you. The vena cava,
and its relationship to the heart, consumes most of your day. Distinction between
artery and vein does not confuse you.
Your interest shifts from blood to mucus
toward nightfall, when you become obsessed
with reading the appearance of sputum.
No doubt your husband shouts: *I don't understand you! I don't understand you at all!*

NOTHING TO OFFER
Doug Self

the keys on my laptop
are full of shit
every time I type
they poop
no letters
no words
just doody stains
on a white page
resembling shitty
Morse code

CHANNELING MIYAGI
Duke Gatsos

Wax on
applied in circles
emits swirls emerge
against black finish cloudy
buffs covering scratches with
murky confusion Confucius say
shine like the sun on Kreese's minions
and their merciless strikes no matter how
evil meeting hate with deft dodges and blocks
mimicking rhythmic moves up under around no
matter how hard I rub blemishes stay to incite hurt
from dumb mistakes like whapping a cement pillar at a
McDonalds drive-thru with my breakaway mirror parallel
parking mishaps dings from stones thrown names
called roadside I fend them off like Danielson
fingerprints on windows touches of people
surface cause pause at the passenger
handle the pull of particular hands
I had the honor to drive sit near
hold lock in private space
all gone in the haze of
memory and wiped
clean to detail
wax off.

JUNE 3ʳᴰ POEM
Doug Jones

He was coming apart.
He liked having somewhere else to be.
He liked how insulated he felt even with an open window.
Outside was different,
different lighting.
He, traveling between outtakes, pretended the doors said "cut" when they closed behind him. He wondered what the actor playing him was like.
He wondered what he was like when the air was the same inside and out.

ELEVEN SEVERED FEET WASH UP
IN THE PACIFIC NORTHWEST

Morgan Adams

Susie found a shoe on the shore. This is a true
story. (Her name wasn't Susie.) She picked up
the shoe and looked under its tongue. Objects have

parts: a shard from a favored cup or a cherry
pie still suggested by the crust's projected
circumference. A piece can identify the whole.

Black trash bags by the side of the road
might be a body, or might be ordinary parts
of a life shed from a truck's bed. Pause frame:

shadows in the leafy backdrop could be a figure
hanging from a noose. Still, the girl not Susie didn't
think a size twelve Reebok running shoe contained

more than grit and seawater. She held it to her
ear for the sound. It was the first of many found
that year: eleven in all, only a few in matching pairs.

FONDNESS
K. Nicole Wilson
    for Tina

I saved a spider with your book
herded him across the living room
and through the French doors
all the pages turning
and turning
on a single leafy leg

ODE TO THE SEMICOLON
Deborah Adams Cooper

I have loved for so long the beauty
mark above your curvy lower lip
Loved your soft eye, a bullet, over your dimpled chin
Wanted to cup your comma,
bring it to my breast

What life force can separate two vital thoughts?
Who is so strong?
What boundaries you set when you are introduced!

Oh, semicolon! From the pages of Jonson
and Shakespeare
you have meted out rhythmic patterns,
brought lover to lover
with your passionate *éclat*

Some call you old-fashioned, middle-class.
Some say you are even 'optional.'
I find you seductive,
dangerously addictive,
a
mysterious
pause.

WITH POETRY
Hap Houlihan

With Poetry,
    1. *Mosquito* can be:
        a. A thinset thicket of thistly bristl;
        b. That high-kneed pesquite youngster;
        c. The Chronic Septopoid Invasion;
        d. The summer renters;
        e. Zziith, troubled hero of *The Malariad* (a sixty-four stanza affair, in which the reign of the Bigslow Smokemakers is finally ended, but at the cost of trillions of her kin);
        f. *Those teeny keening peeple;*
        g. The hemiannual bane of Itchy Nipple, Tennessee;
        h. Mothers of vampire mythos;
        i. Watch-full, Kwicke, & Fearleſſ;

        j. eeeeeeeeeeeeEEEEEEEEE**EEEEEE**

    2. *Joseph McCarthy* can be:
        a. A disease-bearing parasitic insect.

V. At Home

ON GOING HOME
Teneice Durrant

You must have one
to go to. This usually means
your hometown, but I understand this
may be problematic. Everyone has a place,
places, where they grew up, but no one
I love calls Akron, OH home
anymore, so why would I
go back there. Maybe it is the same
for you. An option, then,
is to make a home, one with rooms
full of things, and people, stories
and lives, preferably a good mix of bliss
and devastation.
Then leave it. If you are trying to find
your way home, leaving is a must.

OUT OF A RENTED EXISTENCE
Pamela Gibbs Hirschler

While most girls drew ponies,
she pencil-scratched houses
on the back of first-grade homework

later with a wash of watercolor and ink
drew farm houses and sea cottages
on rough handmade paper,

took to walking small-town streets at night
glimpsing family scenes in picture windows
placed hope in that which she did not hold,

finally found home in a mountain cabin, and
by the grace of a swing on the back porch,
she took root with the peach trees.

ALL I WANT
Jude Lally

is to make it home nights without drawing attention to
myself, before I'm accosted by concerned passersby—
where you trying to go? what can I do?—mostly it's:
going right up the road and *there's nothing you can do*
which seems disappointing news. Sometimes those
offering assistance are unwilling to accept my obstinance:
once I was walked for blocks by two ladies all the way
to my door, or the time I was stopped by a cop who made
me wait while he radioed me a ride. Although I'm glad
people are looking out for me, I wish they'd just let me be.

COUNTRY BREAKFAST
Davina Warner

Grandmother fries bacon
in a coal-black skillet
seasoned from years
of frying chicken
baking cornbread.

Pork fat hisses
against heated iron
spitting grease
onto thin skin
of Grandmother's hands.

With a fork
Grandmother turns shrinking strips
until chewy for me
burnt for Big Daddy
just right
with egg whites swimming in yellow
cinnamon toast
and milk coffee.

UNCLE LEON
Kevin Blankenship

"Sharpen up them spears and knives boys!"
Pause to take a draw of cigarette,
Smoke rises like some mystic shaman.
"Time to cut some tabaccer!"
Another draw, a pause,
Cough following smoke
Like the rattle of a bone cart.
"Do a little dance, up and down them rows,
Swing those arms like a fiddler's draw!"
Then he would stand and call out the rhythm
Like a dance caller, and we would work,
A cadence in tune with earth,
Smell of honeysuckle,
A song of old times,
While Uncle Leon smoked and cut,
Smoked and cut,
Driving us onward
Toward the setting sun.

FAÇADE
Rae Cobbs

Next door's white siding is still warped
by a propane grill's eruption in flames
in the spirit of two twenty-year-olds
left to housesit while a family reunion
roasted my dad. He was dead, but present
so nobody mourned. While we posed
for a photo by the edge of the pool,
in the three-hour time gap my stalwart
son and his wife-to-be rearranged
·the house to prepare for a party.
I've never heard the guest list, but
the house was strangely clean
around them when I walked back in.

Fifteen years later, the siding stands,
background for a painted lady post,
Schefflera, and a Japanese maple,
a sparrow feasting beneath its branches,
and the shadows of the fake boards
almost hide the blemish. Near escape
or mark of passage, the warp stands up
to time, adventure woven into the weft.
I wear respect like peeling paint,
my body warped by injury and wear.
My children monitor their children's
play, masking the ravages in store.

HOMELAND SECURED
Michael Dean Benton

Dragonfly buzzing
Nature's beautiful insect
Or, NSA drone?

OEDIPUS COMPLEX
Patrick Maloney

Mother sent me
down a stream

you open

Love

so i know
a way back

home

HOW A TEACHER PREPARES FOR AN OPEN HOUSE
Jason McKinley Williams

Move the swastika desks to the back of the room.
(I somehow always have 3 or 4)
And while you're at it,
clean up *all* the desk artwork.
Not just the upside-down numerals, crowns, and other gang
    cryptography
you get to
wipe up
every
day,

but every "Jessica loves Dustin 4Ever" and "Slayer"
and even the dragon sketch that shows real talent.
Suitable for framing:

Title: "Irritable Dragon"
Artist: Anonymous Student in Row 2
Medium: No. 2 Pencil on desktop.

Scan the annotated papers on the bulletin board
so you'll remember what examples you have close at hand.

Project your class blog onto the screen.
Pull up your class Facebook page on your phone
(blocked by school filter)
Lay out a stack of index cards with phone, email, and URLs.

Review every "F" and "D" grade quickly
(praying their parents will attend),
review every 88 and 89 grade exhaustively
(knowing their parents will attend),

sit out four chairs in the hallway in case there's a line.
(Sadly, there's never a line).

Open the door,
grateful for every student dragged or dragging,
bite your tongue when the father says: "Yeah, I hated all them essays in
    English, too."

Don't forget
what you do tonight
is also teaching.

JAZZ PERSONAE POEM #19
Elizabeth Beck

Yellow, faded documents
an ancient photo album
all I have to remember

except the scent I spray
from the bottle I did not
know once belonged

to you, my mother I
missed my entire life
not knowing why you left

THE LAST FOREIGN THING
Jessica Swafford

"That's the last foreign
thing I cling to
except my mother,"
he said, declaring
the necessity
for the accent
mark over the
second s
in his name.

"It's under symbols.
I don't know
what it's called,
but it's mine."

GO WHERE MY BODY SAYS GO
Melva Sue Priddy

My most recent mantra:
Do what my body says do;
go where my body says go.
After years of listening to other bodies
I'm finally listening to mine first.
If my body says Yes, it means yes.
If my body says Dig in the earth
rooting out wild violets and crabgrass
from the strawberries until I say Enough,
I obey. If my body says Drink
cold water, I drink cold water.
If my body says Watch
Sound of Music, I watch
Sound of Music. I tolerate bad behavior
less and less & find more and more
of my body to trust. Motion and sweat
and music are the mirrors
my body leans into my body
trust mirrors trust.

WHAT TO DO WHEN YOU'RE LOCKED OUT OF YOUR HOME

Leigh Anne Hornfeldt

You'll want to panic. Don't.
This happens to everyone
and it's important to remember
that you're not alone, not ever
really alone. Can you hear
a lawnmower in the distance,
the rough bark of a dog? Good.

You could pace the perimeter
checking windows and rattling
door knobs, but this is a waste
of time. You lock up. Tight.
You draw the curtains and leave
lights on so whatever it is you think
is trying to get you won't get you.

Step back. Keep stepping back
until your home becomes
a dollhouse and your mother's voice
is pounding in your ears
like a terrified heartbeat. Step back
until your home is a dark pinprick
against the sky. Here you will lose
sound, the lawnmower, the dog,
the mother. This is where you wait.

There is something inside your home
that must come out and you think
you might already know this,
that even the cat knows this as he judges

from the sill each day. Try not to count
how many hours until the door opens.
Pay attention to the sun.
You wouldn't want to burn.

ABOUT THE POETS

Morgan Adams was born and raised in a bookstore in Lexington, Kentucky. She graduated from Berea College and earned her MFA in poetry from Indiana University. Her first chapbook, *In Nonestica*, was released by Accents Publishing in 2013.

Mary Allen lives in Lexington. She comes to poetry through study with poets at the Carnegie Center. In addition to poetry, she writes essays and book reviews and reads extensively in several genres.

Corey Angel is part social worker, part poet. She is currently pursuing a Master of Social Work degree at the University of Kentucky. While originally from Atlanta, Georgia, in her 23 years she has lived in six states, all of which she could call home. Her poems are her history.

Allie Marini Batts is an MFA candidate at Antioch University of Los Angeles, meaning she can explain deconstructionism, but cannot perform simple math. Street Cred: Nominated for Best of the Net & Pushcart Prize. Masthead staff for *Lunch Ticket, Spry Literary Journal, The Weekenders Magazine, Mojave River Review,* and *Bookshelf Bombshells*. Booky-wooks: *You Might Curse Before You Bless* (ELJ Publications); *Unmade & Other Poems* (Beautysleep Press).

Elizabeth Beck lives on a pond with her family in Lexington, Kentucky. She is the author of two books, *insignificant white girl* by Evening Street Press and *Interiors* by Finishing Line Press. She is the founder of the Teen Howl Poetry Series that serves the youth of central Kentucky.

Jennifer Beckett, a poet and teacher, lives in Georgetown. She grew up in Cincinnati but often visited Lexington as a child. Her earliest memories of Lexington include being with her great-grandmother, aunts and uncles. Lexington, in her childhood mind, became the oasis beyond the Ohio River. She still feels that way.

Michelle Benningfield writes, reads, teaches, paints and dances in Lexington where she has lived with her family for six years. She is currently a PhD candidate and teaching assistant at the University of Kentucky and is working on her first historical fiction novel.

Michael Dean Benton sprouted in San Diego, California. Interpolated through Midwest universities. Working the borderline South. Searching for viable alternatives to our sick society. He seeks to give expression to the absurdity of monologic thinking while celebrating the wondrous chaotic creativity of relational thinking, polylogical discourse, polyamorous sexuality, and pantheistic belief.

Kevin Blankenship was born and raised in Breckinridge County, now living in Berea. Proud Kentuckian. Poetry and short fiction have appeared in *The Dead Mule, Pegasus, Zephyrus, Red River Review* and others. His first novel is called *The Ragged Way*. He has a wonderful wife, and great son and stepson.

Sayid R. Bnefsi is 20, attends Berea College, and studies philosophy. He enjoys reading the humanities because it stimulates and refines both his intelligence and ethics. He tries not to pontificate in public, but sometimes cannot resist. His favorite token of poetry is short, but powerfully and well-expressed, poetry.

Maggie Brewer is a native of Worthington, Ohio and first came to Kentucky to attend Transylvania University. She teaches high school history in Danville and lives in Frankfort with her best friend, four cats, a chorkie, and an axolotl.

Kari Burchfield grew up in southeastern Kentucky in a lovely place sandwiched between Cumberland Gap and Pine Mountain. She moved to central Kentucky in 2002 to study English literature and creative writing at the University of Kentucky. She and her husband have a daughter, Piper, and an English Springer Spaniel, Blaze.

Sherry Chandler and her husband, the woodcarver T. R. Williams, have lived on a small farm in Bourbon County, Kentucky for over 30 years. *The Hearth and the Woodcarver*, due out from Wind in early 2014, is a series of poetic meditations on Chandler's relationship with the man and the place.

Writing has been made real for **Rae Cobbs** in Louisville, although she wrote poems in her native California. The first few years were dubious because she wrote in the hope that no one could understand what she meant! She thought her feelings were too dangerous! She loved the poems of Shakespeare, Walt Whitman, and Anne Morrow Lindberg, from her parents—then she loved Marge Piercy, Adrienne Rich, and Sharon Olds on her own. She tries everything from ghazals to blank verse. Her writing time is now or never!

Whitney Collins is the author of *The Hamster Won't Die* and *Hank Is Dead*. She created the humor websites errantparent.com and TheYellowHam.com. Her humor appears on *Salon, The Weeklings, The Huffington Post, Glamour, McSweeney's, Loop,* and *The Big Jewel*.

Deborah Cooper grew up in deep southeastern Kentucky and western West Virginia. She published her first poem in the Huntington High School newspaper when she was 16. She lives in Cynthiana where she enjoys writing, gardening, and playing with her granddaughter, Hazel.

Alison Courtney loves words, loves grammar, loves writing, but hasn't written poetry since that one time in ninth grade. She's probably sold you something at the Morris book shop.

Bront Davis graduated with a degree in English from the University of Kentucky during the last century, but now finds himself doing most of his writing in programming languages.

Bernie DeVille teaches humanities at the Montessori Middle School of Kentucky after a fifteen-year career in bookselling. A lifelong poet, his latest collection, *Many Directions*, is available at the Morris Book Shop. He lives in Lexington with his wife Barbara and his son Julian.

Julian DeVille is a poet of 18 fresh from SCAPA writing at Lafayette High School. When not writing he can be found DJing, biking, gaming, petting cats, and programming computers. Sometimes these things creep into his poetry, sometimes his poetry creeps into them.

Joanie DiMartino is the author of two collections of poetry, *Licking the Spoon* (Finishing Line Press) and *Strange Girls* (Little Red Tree Publishing). She directs the Hidden Treasures Poetry Series and hosts the Soup & Sonnets Literary Salon for Women, where she resides, in Mystic, Connecticut. DiMartino is involved in several collaborative projects with visual artists, and is at work on her next collection.

Marta Dorton is a Lexington painter and printmaker that enjoys the challenges and benefits of writing. She graduated from the University of Kentucky with a studio art degree and worked in graphic arts for 20 years. Her studio space is in Lexington Art League. She is a juried artist in the Kentucky Crafted Program.

Teneice Durrant is a mis-placed Kentuckian trying to find her way home. She is the managing editor of Winged City Chapbook Press and the co-founder and poetry editor for *Blood Lotus*, an online literary journal. She is in love with many things, including chapbooks.

M J Eaton has been awarded 16 grants from the National Endowment to be a Poet in the Schools in Kentucky, Arkansas, Tennessee, and Iowa. Some of that time she was also an Artist in the Schools. She attended Drake University, University of Arkansas, Carolina University of Theology, University of Missouri at Kansas City. Books: *Grab Me a Bus, For Poets, Feeling-My-Way*.

Nettie Farris lives in Floyds Knobs, Indiana. Her work has appeared in *Paperbag, S/tick,* and *Journal of Kentucky Studies*. Her debut collection of poems, *Communion*, is available from Accents Publishing.

Morghan Fuller is a sophomore English teaching major at Eastern Kentucky University and was a 2011 participant of the Young Woman's Writers Project.

Duke Gatsos grew up in Cleveland, Ohio and has been in Lexington for nine years. Two classes taught by Jane Vance at the University of Kentucky gave him the opportunity to have his poems workshopped. From there, he found his way to Poezia and Holler, and his talent and passion for poetry was reborn.

Karen George, author of *Into the Heartland* (Finishing Line Press, 2011) and *Inner Passage* (Red Bird Chapbooks, 2014), has work published in *Memoir, Tupelo Press 30/30 Website, Louisville Review, Permafrost, Wind, Still, Kudzu,* and *Cortland Review*. She holds an MFA in Writing from Spalding University and reviews poetry at *readwritepoetry.blogspot.com*.

Born and raised in Lexington, Kentucky, **Jaria Gordon** is a mother, poet, and endeavoring novelist. She has also attended The Twenty: A Young Writers Advance and was a creative writing student in the summer intensive, the Governor's School for the Arts. She lives and works in Lexington.

Pauletta Hansel's poetry collections include *The Lives We Live in Houses* (Wind Publications) and *What I Did There* (Dos Madres Press). Her poetry and essays appear hither and yon. She leads programs in Cincinnati and beyond, and is Writer-in-Residence at Thomas More College. Pauletta co-edits *Pine Mountain Sand & Gravel*.

Matthew Haughton is the author of *Stand in the Stillness of Woods* (WordTech Editions). His chapbook, *Bee-coursing Box* (Accents Publishing) was nominated for the Weatherford Award for Appalachian Poetry Book of the Year. His poems have appeared in several journals including *The Louisville Review, Still, Border Crossing,* and *The Four Way Review.* Haughton works as a public school teacher in Frankfort, Kentucky.

Pamela Gibbs Hirschler lives and works in Frankfort. Her day job is in information technology, and she writes fiction and poetry. She is a member of the Green River Writers and president of the Kentucky State Poetry Society. She has five children and seven grandchildren, and is a newlywed as well (since April 2013).

Leigh Anne Hornfeldt, a Kentucky native, is the author of *East Main Aviary* and *The Intimacy Archive,* and the editor at Two of Cups Press. Her poem "Laika" placed 2nd in the 2013 Argos Prize Competition (Dorianne Laux, judge). In 2012 she was the recipient of the Kudzu Prize in Poetry.

Hap Houlihan is the manager of the Morris Book Shop. He has been a regular reader at the Holler Poets Series since 2010, and was a featured Holler Poet in June 2012. He lives in Lexington with his family.

Cincinnati native and published poet, **Sue Neufarth Howard** is a member of Greater Cincinnati Writers' League (GCWL). She received the third prize/Honorable Mention in Ohio Poetry Day Contests. Her poems have been published by *High Coupe, Aeqai, Journal of Kentucky Studies, Mid-America Poetry Review, The Incliner—Cincinnati Art Museum.* Her work also appears in *Point Mass,* Summer 2013.

Zachary Johnson is a Maine native who currently lives in Lexington, Kentucky where he works as a psychiatric nurse and writes poetry whenever he is inspired.

Carole Johnston has been writing at least one short poem every day for four years as a spiritual practice, and several of them have been published in both print and online journals. She divides her time between herding poems and wrestling with a novel in progress, both herculean tasks.

Doug Jones makes his home in Lexington. His writing is an attempt to understand dreams and life experiences within the context of the world at large. He is a printmaker, bookbinder, and occasional performer.

Leatha Kendrick leads workshops in poetry and life writing at the Carnegie Center for Literacy and Learning in Lexington, Kentucky. Her fiction, poetry and essays appear widely in journals and anthologies—the result of years of toil and many more rejections than acceptances.

Elizabeth Kilcoyne is an alumni of SCAPA Lafayette and Governor's School for the Arts as a creative writing major. She attends the University of Kentucky as a theater major. During the first week of Lexington Poetry Month she attended The Twenty: A Young Writer's Advance for a second time.

Michelle Knickerbocker grew up in St. Petersburg, Florida and moved to Kentucky in 1995. She lives and works in Frankfort where she graduated from Kentucky State University. She writes poetry, makes jokes, reads, and smiles with her fiancé and their six pets. Life really is good.

Jude Lally fulfills his creative, expressive and therapeutic needs by writing about family, travel, romance, nature, and of course, his disability, a rare neuromuscular condition called Friedrich's ataxia. Although he moved around a lot growing up, he never lived more than 75 miles away from where he currently resides in Lexington, Kentucky.

George Ella Lyon's father read poetry aloud when she was growing up and, while she enjoys all kinds of writing, poetry will always be central to her. Her fourth collection, *Many-Storied House,* was published by the University Press of Kentucky in 2013.

Patrick Maloney has lived in Lexington his entire life. He started writing a little over two years ago. In working with other Lexington poets over the past few months, he has felt growth and motivation to grow as a writer and person. Along with honing procrastination further, he enjoys creating improvisational raps after looking into Medusa's eyes and beholding more of the immeasurable beauty of art.

Born and raised in eastern Kentucky, **Jay McCoy** now lives in Lexington where he spends his days selling books at the Morris Book Shop. He is pursuing his MFA in creative writing through the Bluegrass Writers Studio. Jay's poetry has appeared in several journals and anthologies. He co-founded the Teen Howl Poetry Series.

Christopher McCurry lives in Lexington with his daughter and his wife, where he teaches at Lafayette High School and is a junior editor at Accents Publishing.

Christopher Miller is a Yankee who migrated to the Lexington area in 2004. An avid reader of poetry, he began writing his own verse in early 2012. He is a practicing Buddhist who enjoys reading, meditation, playing guitar, and watching the birds at his feeders.

Jason Lee Miller, MFA, is a development writer at Berea College. His work has appeared in *94 Creations, Blood Lotus, Bluegrass Accolade, The Copperfield Review, Crack the Spine, Danse Macabre du Jour, Dew on the Kudzu, Eunoia Review, FLARE: The Flagler Review, Gloom Cupboard, The Legendary, Milk Sugar, Numinous, Ontologica, State of Imagination, Scarlet Literary, Scissors and Spackle, Subliminal Interiors, The Subtopian,* and *Vine Leaves Literary Journal.* Sporadically, he updates a blog: *offtopic.typepad.com.*

Elane Moore-Turenne was born in Appalachia to teacher parents who loved poetry. She has taught at the University of Kentucky, College of the Bahamas, and Fayette County Schools. She is a University of Kentucky graduate, Phi Beta Kappa, Sullivan Medallion. Her publications include *Vogue's Prix de Paris, Napa Review, The Literature, Macmillan's Anthology of Caribbean Voices, Nassau Voices, Southern Florida, Bahamian Times,* and *Bahamian TV Guide.*

E. K. Mortenson is the author of the chapbooks *The Fifteenth Station* (Accents Publishing, 2012) and *Dreamer or the Dream* (Last Automat Press, 2010), as well as a full-length collection, *What Wakes Us* (Cervena Barva Press, forthcoming). He writes and teaches in Pennsylvania, where he lives with his wife and two children.

Kristine Nowak is originally from Washington but moved to Lexington about five years ago. She has been writing poetry on and off for most of her life but is currently trying to make it a more integral part of each day.

Bronson O'Quinn lives in Lexington, Kentucky, where he writes and participates in the local literary scene. He published a satirical novella in 2012 and is the editor-in-chief of the Accents Publishing Blog. He likes local music, craft beer, and inspired conversation.

Betsy Packard is a New Englander by birth, Kentuckian by choice. She has lived in Leinxgton since 1982. Though her greatest gift is working with animals, with writing—she can't not write. She has been the Mississippi Poetry Society's Poet of the Year, and won an award from the the National Federation of State Poetry Societies (NFSPS), as well as other honors.

Jeremy Dae Paden was born in Italy and raised in Central America and the Caribbean. His poems have appeared in such places as *the Atlanta Review, Beloit Poetry Journal, Cortland Review, The Louisville Review, Naugatuck River Review, pluck!* and *Rattle*. Accents Publishing has recently published *Broken Tulips*. He is an associate professor of Spanish and Latin American literature at Transylvania University and a member of the Affrilachian Poets.

Melva Sue Priddy is a Kentucky writer who has published poetry in *Still: The Journal, The Single Hound, Blood Lotus Journal*, and in anthologies: *Motif 2: come what may, Motif 3: all the livelong day*, and *Bigger Than They Appear: Anthology of Very Short Poems*.

Robin LaMer Rahija is the poetry editor at Rabbit Catastrophe Review.

Jay St. Orts writes the occasional reality-based poem, plays music poorly (but with joy), home-brews, and edits for food and concert money. You can read some of his work, such as his review of The Monkees' semi-barbaric yawp for artistic independence, 1967's *Headquarters* album, at thebrowntweedsociety.com.

Doug Self is a USMC active duty veteran, Operation: Iraqi Freedom veteran, as well as a current Army reservist. He has participated in the Veterans Writing Project: Inaugural Summer Writing Workshop hosted by George Washington University and has completed poetry classes at the Carnegie Center. His work has been published in *Blue Streak: A Journal of Military Poetry* and *0 Dark Thirty*.

Clay Shields calls Lexington home and poetry sustenance; occasionally seen pulled to the side of the street on his bicycle, jotting things down about graffiti, trees, family, friends.

Vijay Singh is a dreamer-poet (more of a dreamer, less of a poet) who writes poems on the weekends and in leisure hours. He studied electrical engineering at University of Minnesota and now lives and works in Lexington.

Savannah Sipple is from Beattyville, Kentucky and is currently working on a collection of persona poems set in one small Appalachian town. Her work has been featured in *Now and Then, Appalachian Heritage, The Louisville Review, New Southerner,* and *Motif 3: All the Livelong Day.* She writes about poetry at *StructureAndStyle.tumblr.com.*

Born outside Seattle, Washington, **G.A. Smith** has lived in his paternal family roots of Central Kentucky since 2000. An alumnus of both the Governor's School for the Arts (2007) and The Twenty (2011-2013), his work has been featured in *pluck!, The Lumberyard,* and *Still: The Journal.*

Kate Spencer was born and raised in the prairies of the Midwest, but has begun to call Lexington home after living here for the past eight years. She is a psychologist by education, training, and profession, but a writer, artist, and seeker at heart.

Affrilachian Poet and Cave Canem Fellow, **Bianca Spriggs** is a multi-disciplinary artist who lives and works in Lexington, Kentucky. The recipient of a 2013 Al Smith Individual Artist Fellowship in Poetry, Bianca is the author of *Kaffir Lily* and *How Swallowtails Become Dragons.* In partnership with the Kentucky Domestic Violence Association, she is the creator of *The SwallowTale Project,* a creative writing workshop designed for incarcerated women. She also serves as the current managing editor of *pluck! The Journal of Affrilachian Arts & Culture.*

Keith Stewart splits his time between his hometown of Hyden and the great city of Lexington, Kentucky. He prefers humor over seriousness, kindness over angst, and chili cheese Fritos over plain. His blog can be found at *astrongmanscupoftea.blogspot.com.*

Karah Stokes teaches English for a living, but gardening is her religion. Writing poetry and singing are addictions she has never been able to get completely free of.

Katerina Stoykova-Klemer is the author of three poetry books, most recently *The Porcupine of Mind* (Broadstone Books, 2012). Katerina is the founder of poetry and prose groups in Lexington, Kentucky. She hosts *Accents* radio show on WRFL, 88.1 FM, Lexington. In January 2010, Katerina launched Accents Publishing.

Jessica Swafford is a student at Berea College, a poet for over 20 years, and a lifelong lover of learning.

Rudy Thomas is the editor and publisher of Old Seventy Creek Press. He has published 24 books of his own, mostly poetry, but also three novels and a book of short stories. He has published more than 800 poems, articles, and short stories in magazines and journals. He is ancient enough to have won the Jesse Stuart Award for poetry when Stuart was alive.

Beatrice Underwood-Sweet, despite stints living in both California and (currently) Oklahoma, is and always will be a Kentuckian! She teaches special education to pay the bills. She finds inspiration in community, in the mundane, and sometimes in the tragic.

Davina Warner writes daily for her job as a social worker, but creative writing and journaling have been her life's blood since childhood. She's currently writing a memoir about her relationship with her mother. At Carnegie Center classes she has found inspiration, guidance and community with local writers.

Jason McKinley Williams is a software developer, erstwhile high school English teacher, erstwhile writer, erstwhile whatever else interested him at the time. His work has been published in *Appalachian Heritage, Kudzu, Public Republic,* and a few other places.

K. Nicole Wilson attempts to merge sports and poetics in a manner as palatable to the masses as a game-winning field goal. She founded the inKY reading series, has appeared as a feature at Holler Poets Series, Stone Soup Poetry Series, Molly Malone's Reading Series and as a Gypsy Poet at the Kentucky Women Writers Conference.

Elle Wong, Appalachian by accident and writer by necessity, is a Taiwanese American, queer, feminist poet from Lexington and Berea. A survivor of mishaps and circumstance, her writing is borne out of complex love—love of family, of Kentucky, of food, and of self.

Marianne Worthington is co-founder and poetry editor of *Still: The Journal* and poetry editor of *Now & Then: The Appalachian Magazine*. Her poetry collection, *Larger Bodies than Mine*, won the 2007 Appalachian Book of the Year Award. She lives in Williamsburg, Kentucky.

Tyler Worthington was born at Central Baptist Hospital in Lexington, Kentucky. Although he grew up with ties to an extended family in Frankfort and Versailles, Kentucky as well as Blacksburg, Virginia and the county of Cuba in upper New York State, he grew up attending school in Lexington.

ABOUT THE EDITORS

Hap Houlihan is the manager of the Morris Book Shop. He has been a regular reader at the Holler Poets Series since 2010, and was a featured Holler Poet in June 2012. He lives in Lexington with his wife Lori and his sons Murphy and Simon.

Christopher McCurry lives in Lexington, Kentucky with his daughter and his wife, where he teaches high school English and is a junior editor at Accents Publishing. His poems have appeared in *Limestone, The Los Angeles Review, Rabbit Catastrophe* and others. His short story, "Those Who Trespass Against Us," won the *Still: The Journal's* 2013 fiction contest. He is working on a master's degree in English literature, thanks to a fellowship from the CE&S Foundation, at the Bread Loaf School of English.

www.ingramcontent.com/pod-product-compliance
Lightning Source LLC
Chambersburg PA
CBHW030330080526
44584CB00012B/797